Embracing
a Concrete
Desert

Text copyright © Lynne E. Chandler 2010
The author asserts the moral right
to be identified as the author of this work

Published by
The Bible Reading Fellowship
15 The Chambers, Vineyard
Abingdon OX14 3FE
United Kingdom
Tel: +44 (0)1865 319700
Email: enquiries@brf.org.uk
Website: www.brf.org.uk

BRF is a Registered Charity

ISBN 978 1 84101 686 3

First published 2010
10 9 8 7 6 5 4 3 2 1 0

A catalogue record for this book is available from the British Library

Printed in Singapore by Craft Print International Ltd

Embracing a Concrete Desert

A spiritual journey towards wholeness

Lynne E. Chandler

To Paul-Gordon Chandler,
my husband and soulmate

'In your presence I have bloomed into me'

Acknowledgments

My thanks to…

*Madeleine Downey and Barbara Comar,
for your enthusiastic, encouraging spirits*

*St John's Church and the 'people flowers' of Cairo,
pilgrims on the journey*

*My family: Paul-Gordon, Britelle, Treston,
for your laughter, tears and sustaining presence*

Dad and Mom, for your generous, loving support

*Naomi Starkey, my Commissioning Editor,
for your vision, heart and expertise*

Contents

Introduction

These pages were brought to birth during a modern-day Middle Eastern fight for survival. During my first two years in Cairo I felt as if I was sharing a dried-up desert well, abandoned with Joseph and his coat of many colours. My soul dehydrated as I grieved the loss of nature and quiet and freedom. In time I discovered that the poisonous thorn piercing through my camel saddle had a name—negativity. Since I had been robbed of outward resources, such as morning walks in fresh air, I was forced to accept that the alternative to dying spiritually was to learn to manoeuvre within. My soul was being shaken awake from a slumber of security and self-centredness. It wasn't like an alarm clock going off or a loud mosque call blasting, but like the gentle blowing in of a cool spring breeze, hardly perceptible at first.

The deeper I searched, the more strongly I was drawn to my Creator, the essence of all being. Layers and layers of grime had built up but at the core rested God's image. Stories of Jesus introduced themselves to me differently. They hinted at what God looked like, wearing Middle Eastern shoes, of course. What Christ found important and essential, he communicated through the way he lived his life, but I'm sure much was lost on his friends then, as now. Living faith, transformation, being alive to the present moment—these were things worth embracing and nurturing in others through an outwardly focused life. Slowly my heartstrings began to retune to the source of all life. Creation, I learned, includes 'people flowers'. My Cairo garden had nearly 20 million of them.

The first leap I took was decided by my mind. I chose to take it; then my heart was persuaded to follow. There was a lot of dramatic jerking and sputtering and stumbling along—what a sight I was at times! This book is the story of some of that journey, as it is not finished yet. Because it's not about arriving, I have learnt that I don't have to wait till the end to celebrate. What follows is simply a glimpse of raw wanderings through the barren lands of concrete and the discovery of fresh water springs of the soul.

- 1 -

When life gives you smog, enjoy the sunsets

If someone had told me at any other point in my life that I would end up living in one of the most polluted cities in the world, I would have laughed in terror. In fact, I had already visited the exotic, historic city of Cairo twice in my life and hated it both times. How could someone possibly live in such a place of chaos, pollution, constant noise and no nature? It could not be survivable—and certainly no one would ever choose to be put there; they would have to be born into it. I'm not saying this perspective is a good one. It is just my own honest, desperate opinion and I hope it holds no truth for any of my millions of neighbours.

If you know the great story of Jonah, then you'll understand where I'm coming from. I love to come across these far-out stories when I'm reading the Bible. It's like finding a mirror sticking out from between the printed words. Well, maybe I only love it when there's a sense of recognition, when I'm debriefing myself after having (sort of) survived a similar messy story in my own life. Sometimes I wonder why I can't have the same 'mirror' experience with something less dramatic, like sitting by quiet waters, restoring my soul.

Jonah. I knew from the first words out of my husband Paul-Gordon's adventuresome mouth that I'd be facing the choice between following quietly or buying a boat ticket for the fastest route away from Nineveh—I mean, Cairo—with the risk that I'd be spat up there anyway, but all yucky-mucky-like, after unnecessary self-inflicted suffering. I guess it must have been, at the very least, embarrassing for the prophet, having to jump into a swirling sea-storm to save an endangered boat, knowing that it was all his fault.

Now, I'm definitely the thrill-seeking type, so it wasn't the Egyptian archaeology, adventure desert caravanning or *Death on the Nile* images that were scaring me; it was the 'big developing world city' thing.

So I thought I would try to get past the whole 'not me' Jonah story, and follow. I'm actually quite good at following, sometimes. It wasn't as if going to pastor an international church was an off-the-wall cause. It was a dream for both of us, something deeper and more spiritually fulfilling than what we were doing at the time. My husband, not I, was going to be the pastor but I would be involved too, beyond just coordinating music for services. As for being a full-time mum and bad housewife (not a bad wife, I mean, but the 'house' bit), I knew I could do that anywhere in the world. Putting aside the large 'pollution-and-lack-of-nature phobia' badge I was wearing mentally, I knew everything would be OK because this opportunity was a 'call'—or something like that. I knew lots of people who had had 'calls' before and I sometimes wished I had a special one of my own, but mine seemed to be a generalised sort of calling that I could fulfil anywhere—the call to journey towards God and celebrate the divine spark in others. I knew that this could keep me out of trouble for a lifetime.

To make a long story short, we sold our house and gave away our family dog, which expert people had said would never survive the harshness of the city—not because of the pollution but because of the risk of being poisoned (a common way to rid the streets of stray dogs). We put all our earthly belongings into storage, including my concert harp, and headed off for the Middle East. It was just after the events of 9/11 but people were usually polite in their best wishes for our safety and their response to our decision to uproot our eleven-year-old daughter, Britelle, and eight-year-old son, Treston.

Thankfully we were welcomed with open arms by the beautiful little church in Cairo, whose people were happy to have anyone filling the post—even better a family with children and a pastor who loved to write and deliver sermons. The church property also hosted ten other congregations, worshipping in a variety of other languages: several in Arabic, French, Korean, Swedish and a couple of African languages.

— ❊ —

Eighteen months after our arrival, I had gone through all the culture shock, used all the adjustment strategies, shed gallons of tears and offered great quantities of wordless prayers, but I was still struggling. It wasn't that I was unhappy with my life's purpose. I had made friends, and I enjoyed leading a musical ensemble at church and facilitating a monthly church book club. Everyone else in the family was thriving at the time. Why couldn't I adjust?

Then, one day in March, I made a promise to my family during dinner that I would never say another bad word about living in a big, polluted, nature-void city, or they could make me pay them ten Egyptian pounds. The poison of negative thinking was overtaking even my smog-induced asthma problem. So I made a positive decision to put on a pair of negative-free glasses that cold March morning, and slowly I started to see beautiful sunsets through the smog. They really are red and mysterious-looking—the sunsets, that is, not the glasses. Next I discovered that sunrises look nice through smog, too. Then the little birds that I was feeding on my windowsill began to look happier, and the large sycamore tree generously blocking the view of the office building next door started having leaves that danced in the wind, reminding me of God's Spirit blowing life and hope my way—if only I'd notice. I had to pay up once for a negative slip in attitude, but that was four months into the deal.

One of my best friends here is a Buddhist and she instructed me in calm breathing, which helped with my asthma but also helped me go deeper in my own Christian faith, meditating on the beautiful words of scripture and being mindful of God in the little things in life, like recognising nature in my heart and 'people flowers'. The concept of a garden full of people, rather than flowers, bloomed into an important image for me. It opened up my mind and heart to search for beauty in others. I also discovered the 19th-century American poet Emily Dickinson by accident and tried my hand at some 'poem therapy'.

The other day, I remembered one thing I had learnt in Year 6 from the decorations around my classroom, back in the Chicago area. One wall was plastered with cut-out paper lemons and bubble letters saying, 'If life gives you lemons, make lemonade.' I always liked working at lemonade stands. I wonder what smog-ade would taste like!

I wish I could say that I have arrived and will never have to stare into the darkness of my own pyramid sarcophagus chamber again, but I know that isn't so. I do know, though, that I have to embrace the present moment and celebrate life, whatever that may involve today. My Creator is alive within and throughout this amazing world, and has never failed, through thick and thin, to wrap me in wings of protection and comfort. There are many layers of negativity to be peeled back so that a glimpse of God's image can show through. Just as one layer is lifting, another appears to take its place. That's where grace comes in. In desperate times, God dishes it out lavishly, like my grandma's generous servings of homemade strawberry shortcake. It's admittedly smoggy in my heart sometimes but there are sunsets worth celebrating, too. Reading and thinking about Jesus and how he lived have definitely pointed me in the right direction.

— ❧ —

I don't know where I'm at in the Jonah story now. Maybe I'm just trying to come to terms with the worm-eaten vine, like Jonah outside the gates of Nineveh. At least he got to sit somewhere quiet to complain! One day God provided a vine to shade him and the next day a worm destroyed it (see Jonah 4). I hope I'll be able to move on to something more exciting, like imagining myself as the woman who anointed Jesus' feet with perfume (Mark 14:3–9) or wondering if I'm Martha or Mary (Luke 10:38–42). But in the meantime, trying to look and live deeply one day at a time is my calling—that, and enjoying sunsets in smog.

My sister in Cairo

I don't know what hunger is,
but my sister in Cairo does.
I don't know how poverty pains,
but my brother here shows me the way.

Why was I born to richness of choices?
Why were they born without?

Somehow there must be a way to bridge
the chasm that comes between.

The clay that formed our souls was God's;
there's no difference between you and me.
Blessed are the poor in spirit.
I have much to learn from them.

I'll gladly give you my earthly treasures
if you give me some of heaven.

- *2* -

Ismeen

Just a few days into our Cairo adventure, we met a little girl probably about my son Treston's age. That evening, she was begging for money, effectively communicating her hopes of not having to go to bed hungry. Unfortunately I did not have any *gineeh* (Egyptian pounds) on me and my husband had wandered off in another direction. Directly behind me, I found that the pavement was being transformed into a place of worship. The call to prayer had not yet sounded but was clearly expected soon. I fought to lower my voice as I explained in English, and in vain, that I didn't have any money with me. Pulling out one of my new Arabic phrases, I asked her what her name was. Her deeply sunken brown eyes gazed at me in confusion and apprehension. I smiled and talked to her gently but she could not return my smile. 'Ismeen,' she whispered.

The ragged, oversized, long-sleeved woollen dress she was wearing looked unbearable in the oppressive July heat. She carefully inspected the perfectly clean, barely worn clothes of my children. Her eyes stopped on Treston's tennis shoes. She studied them for a long time and then inconspicuously glanced down at her own dirty, calloused, bare feet. I wondered if I should wrestle his shoes off him and hand them over.

Behind me the prayers grew louder. I tried to tell Ismeen I would be right back and went in search of my husband. He was finally found, talking to a vendor who had not stopped to pray. Quickly my children told him that we needed money to give to Ismeen. 'Who is Ismeen?' 'Our new friend,' they explained. By the time we emerged from the twists and turns of the bazaar shops, prayer time had ended. Ismeen was gone.

Poverty

Poverty looked me in the face today.
She smiled
and made a plea.
How could I turn my eyes away,
when she reflected
me?
A refrain of thankfulness is stuck
repeating in my head.

Will I one day search for it,
when circumstances
change,

and find the melody off tune,
or
that it's set me
free?

The sounds, the smells

I can't escape the
sounds, the smells.
Assault is everywhere.

I wish it did not drain me so,
But this is how

you made me.

3

Have you ever lived through a sandstorm and not tasted grit in your teeth?

Have you ever experienced a desert caravan crossing (whether in real life or in your spirit)? The end is in sight and you assume you'll soon get to rest in the shade of a palm tree for a very long while—maybe even drink from the pure cool centre of a fresh water spring for as long as your heart desires. You will have earned it. Your throat will have earned it. Your body's natural salt reserves have long ago been sweated into evaporation. In place of the ancient wandering Hebrews' focus on a pillar of cloud by day and a pillar of fire by night, you're swatting black horseflies by day and unwillingly donating blood to giant mosquitoes by night. Saddle sores and permanently hobbled legs have been bestowed upon you with your faithful camel's blessing. It's time to rest—to refresh, to dream of water pouring from a rock, manna and quail in the wilderness and the absence of plaguing locusts. Little do you know that the sandstorms are brewing.

I don't know about sandstorms in other parts of the world, but here in Egypt they are something to brace yourself for. These storms are called *khamseens*, taken from the Arabic word for 'fifty'. *Khamseens* are not like individual tornadoes, quick and painful and deadly. They are more like a tornado marathon contest that lasts for 50 days, give or take a few. In such a contest, points are awarded to whichever storm can blow the hardest and longest, and wreak the most havoc on unsuspecting and inexperienced visitors. If you are a camel, you are OK; God gave you special eyelids to zip shut, tiny ears and thick but flexible lips and nostrils that seal as well. If you are not a camel, then you have a lot of trouble ahead of you.

Prepare yourself for your symptoms: grit in your teeth, your eyes, your hair and everywhere. Next come wheezy breathing, coughing and the general feeling that a camel's hoof is pushing your ribs through your chest while your lungs are squeezed by his nasty slimy lips. Oh, and sleepless nights. All these symptoms are well within the range of normal sandstorm fallout. Dusting your coffee table daily is futile—and, whatever you do, do not bother washing your unsealed, uninsulated windows until the season officially passes.

Survival skills: first of all, you need to refocus and be thankful that you do not live in a tent. Also, be thankful that you have access to water for cleaning up the grit. Another bonus worth celebrating is that you don't have to dust or clean very often because it's actually kind of cool to see how thick the build-up of this fine, sticky, well-travelled sand can get. You can enjoy writing finger messages to your children in its layers on the table. You will also have an excuse to practise your meditation and breath-calming techniques, which will be useful to draw on during non-sandstorm season, too.

It truly is an adventure to pick up your children from school when the sky is dark with looming swirls. You have to rush home to safety with your faces carefully covered and then listen to the symphony of blowing grains pummelling your windowpanes. If you are lucky, you will hear the whistle of sand sonatas through your apartment's lift shaft (which adjoins your kitchen and bathrooms for your listening pleasure). If the Sahara is really trying to impress you, she will even knock out your electricity, so you can huddle together by candlelight and tell each other stories. Those stories will remind you of past seasons and tell you if this is the worst one you've ever seen. Remember the year when the lamp got knocked over and you all screamed? And, although it's no fun to live with scratched eyeballs and gritty teeth, you know it soon will pass.

The year I moved to Cairo, I felt as if a sandstorm had hit my life—but it went on and on and on. By the time 50 days had multiplied by ten, I was in panic mode. Would it ever end? Well, as it happens, just on the verge of my emotional breaking point, it all suddenly calmed. I think Jesus must have been riding on his donkey at the pyramids nearby and noticed I was tipping past what I could humanly handle, even with all the outpourings of divine intervention that I knew were sustaining me.

So, at that point my body and soul got to go on a wonderful holiday, running through fields of well-watered flowers and twirling in tall wild prairie grass. Summer had arrived and our family was able to return to our flat near Chicago to rest. I was given a short but perfect hiatus, until I returned to Cairo and the emotional storms hit again. Life's desert winds came from a different direction this time and all I could do was hang on and on and on. I did manage to survive the storm but I emerged exhausted, with teeth full of sandy grit.

As the storm calmed, little did I know that this was only a brief stop at an oasis with a chance to rest, but only in the eye of the storm. Wow! Things were getting out of hand. The next storm to blow in was sudden. It hit me and showed no mercy. I felt as if it had tossed me up into a date palm tree; it mangled me and crushed me, and I thought I was a goner for sure. I'd heard about storms like this one but never thought I'd see one in my lifetime. Yet, this time something different was in the air. What looked so impossible to face brought Jesus back on his donkey. I guess he was just hanging out nearby, behind the Sphinx in Giza, until I realised I needed divine help to survive. I had thought, with all those years of storm fighting under my belt, that I could handle at least one on my own.

What I'd thought was the beginning of the mother of all sandstorms—like someone knocking me off my feet with a truck full of sand—was just some friends throwing sand into my eyes, accidentally. What were they thinking? They might have realised, with all the storms I'd had to survive, that I was already near the breaking point. They said they were sorry, though; it was a mistake. Now they were offering their hands to lift me back up and dust me off.

One minute I felt like throwing sand back at them and the next I felt like burrowing out of sight, but neither action would have moved me into a place of peace and safety. While I was standing there, vacillating with sand fever, I was handed two gift boxes from God (as if I could hold *anything* then!). One was labelled 'Time' and the other 'Grace'. But I thought I'd already passed the course on forgiveness and the one on patience, years ago. I thought I had the gifts of time and grace. Those didn't have an expiry date, did they?

The hands of my friends were still there, offering to lift me out. 'Forget it!' I wanted to shout. 'You're the last ones I want to help me out. You pushed me in! What if you do it again?' Then I could feel God's embrace. I was no longer alone, a victim of sandy misery. I was given the strength to accept help from those who had hurt me. The process would take time but digging me out, one handful of sand at a time, would eventually free me.

As my friends took turns with the shovel, I held those gifts— time; grace. As I began to unwrap them, a gentle gush of fresh air (clean, gritless, unpolluted air) brushed over my face. The decision had been made: I would let go of the pain and forgive. The course had been set toward healing.

Rest would come. Peace had already arrived. If or when life pointed the way, I would climb down and help to dig someone else out, with the faithful guidance of my Creator's ever-sustaining presence. And, when the waves of sand kicked up once more and a new storm came, I was sure that I would be brushed off again and again and again.

Holding on

I'm holding on with
all my might
but slowly my grip is
slipping.
I have to meet despair
again—
if only it'd stop calling my name!

Holding on

A desert caravan

I joined a desert caravan.
It would take several years to cross.

What I imagined to be adventure
over rolling seas of sand
quickly turned to wilderness,
a dry and barren land.
Mirages of wells and oases plagued me,
saddle sores and tears.
My fitful dreams were forced to change.
I had to trust my Guide.
He'd led many a caravan this way.
He would bring me to the other side.

My heart began to listen to my camel's story;
she had much to teach me of faith.
Perfectly designed for this very journey:
eyes, ears, nose and hooves.
No detail forgotten in her Maker's planning,
she willingly carried me.
Did I, as well, have gifts to fit me for this journey?
I would have to search within.

caravan

4

Ayad

We first met Ayad by telephone. The morning after our move to Egypt, the ringing of the phone tried to rouse us from our jetlagged blur. Air conditioners effectively blocked the outdoor sounds of blaring music, car horns and voices, even dulled the roar of the train barrelling past our apartment. Eventually the persistent ring woke us from our slumber. At the other end of the line was a cheery, welcoming Egyptian voice, asking for 'Father'. I reminded the caller that Father Barry had returned to Australia but, yes, I thought Father Paul-Gordon would be more than happy to receive his calls at 10am each morning.

Three days later, we met Ayad at church. He welcomed us with great enthusiasm and we began to collect his story. Now probably in his late 40s, Ayad had suffered for many years from some sort of mental illness. He had lived in America for a while but was not given long-term residency so he returned to Egypt to live with his brother. He could not hold down a job and seemed to survive off a form of Egyptian food stamps and the family's help, it being the duty of his elder brother to care for him. His life's purpose revolved around our church. The priest in charge always held his passport and money in safe keeping for him, giving them to him as requested in times of need.

We had arrived at church an hour early to set up for our very first worship service. There was Ayad, waiting to help. It was heart-warming to see how well integrated he was by the congregation, as a valued member of the family. When after-church dinners were planned, someone was always sure to include Ayad and pay for his portion. He regularly called many other members of the congregation, as well as us, simply to check in during the week to see how they were doing.

One Tuesday morning, Ayad called as usual. Paul-Gordon was at home, working at a desk strewn with books and notes, deep in his sermon preparation. Ayad wanted to remind him of something to be included in the next week's bulletin and to see if 'Father' needed any help. Paul-Gordon said he thought things were OK for the day, but could he do anything for Ayad? No, all was well. His last words, as always, were 'Praise be to Jesus.'

Several days passed. We commented at the end of the week that we hadn't heard anything from Ayad, and we made a mental note to call him. As the country of Egypt follows the Islamic weekend schedule, Friday and Saturday are days off, so our weekly worship service is held on Saturday. The time for Saturday evening service arrived and, surprisingly, Ayad was not there early to help set things up. Maybe he was sick. We decided to call him as soon as we got home.

When Paul-Gordon called that evening, Ayad's brother answered the phone. Paul-Gordon asked to speak with Ayad, and his brother immediately explained that he knew who Father Paul-Gordon was but hadn't known how to contact him. He said that Ayad had died four days earlier. A massive heart attack on Tuesday night had ended his life—the last day that Paul-Gordon had heard his voice.

Ayad was a gift to our little congregation. He had given of himself to us all.

An oasis in the din

Our little church, St John the Baptist,
an oasis in the din
of honking cars, polluted air,
and noise churning within.
A much sought-after refuge I find
when quietly I come
to worship each week with those who are
my pilgrim friends of the way.
As we raise our voices with the company of heaven,
with those who've gone before,
as we share bread and wine profound
praise lifts from our souls.

Guide us into your arms, dear Lord.

We are not confined to a building,
to see your presence in our world.
Teach us to celebrate your gifts with thankful hearts.
May glory to you be given.

-5-

On adopting a city

Waging an inner battle against an ancient city is a really bad idea. I don't recommend it to anyone. The city is a lot bigger and older than you are, a lot more indifferent to individual struggles, and you won't win. In fact, it's a waste of your time.

If you ever find yourself wanting to run from such a problem, I suggest you make friends with the city instead. Invite it to tea or to dinner. Don't expect it to bring you flowers. Don't expect it to bring you a box of your favourite chocolates. Unless this city has invited you to evaluate the status of its rubbish collection system, its smog levels or the treatment of some of its inhabitants, or plans to replace anything remotely green with concrete, then you need to keep your mouth shut tightly. If your mouth is shut tightly, then no one will get hurt. Soon your brain will cooperate and start to look for good things to celebrate.

If someone in this city is unkind to you, remember the little old man who sits by the fruit stand on *Shera Tessa* (Road Nine), who offered you a chair to sit on when you were waiting for the bakery to open. If that doesn't help, remember the little old woman with the deep brown wrinkles, who sits on the pavement by the mosque every Friday. Or how about the little children who don't go to school but follow you around as if you were the Pied Piper until you hand over the lollipops that they know from experience are in your handbag?

These kinds of situations need to be embraced, not rejected.

A place, like a person, needs to feel accepted by you. Why not think about adopting it? If you decide that's a good idea, you will eventually stop telling yourself how hard it is to love. Instead you will learn to love it. Why not? Maybe you could even think of some ways to make it happier. No one will tell you that that is a waste of time.

One day, after you have been nice to your city for quite a while, you will wake up and find that it likes you. It might not tell you it's happy that you have adopted it, but your heart will know it was a good idea. If the layer of smoggy misery on your heart starts to disappear, the sun can shine straight in. And if the sun shines straight in, your heart will smile and grow bigger and you will start to feel as if you live in a field of beautiful flowers—people flowers. Every one of these flowers in your adopted city may look different but you are all interconnected, created by God. The great Gardener of the flowers is very happy with his work: he has done a good job. He has brought you to this city to live among them and you are now one of its flowers, too.

Wings of escape

I wish I could fly on a
magic carpet,
to a place where stress
doesn't reign.
Today my dreams are my
wings of escape;
your creation is my
longing.
Just to sit at your feet
in the quiet of a field,
allowing my senses
refreshment.
For now I'm confined to the
cage of a building
but your birds bring me news of
beyond.

- 6 -

Alive to the moment

Taking refuge from the assault of toxic fluids being used to renovate the apartment above us, I write sealed into a room with an air purifier attempting to win the battle. It is, in reality, impossible to shut oneself off from the world, which crushes in everywhere in this foreign wilderness. Cairo windows don't seal; fan mountings in kitchens and bathrooms effectively waft in every variety of smells and sounds in the course of a day. So my asthmatic coughing continues, calm breathing is mandated and I gather together determination and inner resolve, my usual resources, to keep despair at bay. On days like these it is tempting but futile to question how and why I've arrived at this moment in time. This, too, shall pass. Foundations within are being shaken but not destroyed. God is sowing a garden in my heart that will hereafter grant me yet deeper reflections on his presence in the cathedral of creation, as I am learning to find his divine image in concrete deserts and people. Will a day ever pass again when I am not profoundly grateful for the glimpse of a tree or the sound of a bird's call as it celebrates the discovery of food for its family and friends?

I live. I am alive to the moment. I breathe in harmony with my surroundings. My world of nature here is small, very small. Today it consists of the sycamore tree outside the window of my bedroom, the one that blocks my view of the office building next door. Sunlight is dancing off those blowing leaves,

God's breath reminding me of divine presence. I am safe in the moment. This is where I am to be. I rest in silence but my inner spirit is bursting with song, a song of thanksgiving for God's deliverance. Emotions come and go like waves breaking on a sandy Red Sea beach. Some melt back into the whole; others grow to dramatic heights; but they come, they go. I must not forget the essence of those emotional waves—the water beneath, the source of life and strength, beautiful and endless.

I am very thankful for this tree outside my window. Car horns are honking, the train blasting by, security guards arguing on the pavement, dust blowing, but my tree stands tall; always sensitive to the blowing wind, its branches dance freely. Its roots are strong, stretching down to feed from the deep source of the Nile's excess, reaching full and high toward the smog-hidden sun and the sky. It has not lived a life in vain. It has inspired me like a burning bush, so that my spirit is pointed toward its Creator, my Creator, and we are one in a voice of praise. As God fed Elijah not far from here in the Sinai peninsula with the help of the ravens (1 Kings 17:5–6), so I am being fed in spirit with the help of this dusty old tree and the little sparrows that play on my front windowsill. It is enough.

Dreams are good when they pull you toward hope, but being satisfied in the present moment, satisfied with what I've been given, is receiving the gift of hope here and now. God sees the depths of my heart, his mighty wings surround me, and today that presence has been revealed through the beauty of a common tree. It is no mere tree, now, but a window, an icon, a holy moment reflected. I am thankful for this gift for the journey; I need no more in the present.

Good morning tree

Good morning tree, my faithful friend.
A new day has begun.
Your leaves keep rhythm with
the wind as with the breath of God's Spirit.
Shafts of light,
the gift of sun,
God's presence lights the day.

tree

– 7 –

Other children's lives

My children were complaining of boredom the other week-end. I persuaded them to play some board games. As we were setting things up, we heard the familiar clip-clop of a donkey cart, right outside our window. We glanced out and saw two young boys, no more than ten years old. They were driving a cart overloaded with rubbish that they had probably been collecting since early morning. As they pulled up to the building next door, they found bins overflowing, waiting to be emptied. The contents would be taken by these children back to their parents, who live with them in what is known as The Village of Garbage, in Cairo's district of Mokkattam. There the valuable process of sorting, recycling and disposal would begin.

Mokkattam will emerge again, later in my reflections. It is a place of paradox—physically filthy but spiritually beautiful. To visit the homes of the children who live there is both heart-wrenching and inspiring. The glaring need for compassionate assistance to these rubbish collectors and their families has captured the hearts of many people, and now schools, medical assistance, places of worship and a viable recycling centre all exist within this 'rubbish village'.

Half of the rubbish the children outside my window were assigned to collect was in the bins. The other half carelessly littered the ground. Both boys scampered down from their cart and began the tedious task of picking up the strewn waste.

The donkeys were wearing blinkers to prevent them from distraction. They waited patiently. Armed security guards from the building stood over the boys, refusing even a smile.

I looked back at my two well-fed, well-clothed, bored children, who had witnessed the scene with me. They commented on the underfed donkeys and how dangerous the work must be for the boys, who had no shoes to wear. Complaints of boredom vanished. The young boys finished their task, climbed back on to their cart and turned their donkeys toward the next building.

Donkeys were the first local animals to capture my heart. Their eyes are so kind and trusting. Our church supports a wonderful donkey protection organisation, run by an old Muslim veterinarian here. Through his work we are able to provide humane harnesses, training on the importance of daily food and fresh water, and veterinary care to families throughout Cairo. So many lives depend on the health and longevity of their donkeys.

A Middle Eastern donkey

To be born a Middle Eastern donkey—
some say it is a curse.
He hobbles the streets with sores from
whips
swung by those who do not care.

Enabling livelihood
is all that's on their owners' minds.
Beasts of burden to help, but always more children to feed:
when will the cycle of poverty end?

I caught his eye as he limped by one day—
grace,
endurance,
pride.

It was a Middle Eastern donkey
That my Lord chose to ride.

– 8 –

On embracing grey hair and fat deposits

Twenty years ago I would have found this topic appalling to ponder. Who on earth could be happy that their hair was discolouring—I mean, greying? Why would anyone stop fighting their unique genetic make-up and embrace fat deposits? OK, maybe in another culture where the aged are revered and fat dimples are a sign of being loved and well cared for, but they are an affront to a 21st-century Western mindset. If we could adopt that 'other culture's' view, what a strike it would be against the values of materialism, the assumptions of self-focus and superficial concern!

Living in Egypt for some years now, where we 21st-century folk are still puzzling over how the ancient pyramids really were engineered, I have been given the opportunity to step back from the frenzy of 'more, newer, better' and look a bit deeper from time to time—on days when I am paying attention, that is. This is a place where the latest BMW has to decide whether to rev past a crumbling donkey cart and driver or respectfully yield the right of way and be 60 seconds later to an important appointment. That kind of sight makes you stop and think, especially when the BMW's decision is usually to blast past in a fury of self-absorption.

A flock of sheep being herded through the city streets of Cairo during the Islamic holy month of Ramadan is a completely different story. You can beep your horn all you want, or roll down your window and yell in frustration at the shepherd, but you will be forced to sit back and wait. You can do it patiently and take pleasure in the sight of rural meeting urban—the jostling of dusty wool, the sounds of baaing and maybe even *some* of the smells. Of course, if you're a vegetarian, as I am, it will take some extra creative suppression to enjoy the scene and not get obsessive about the 'destined for slaughter' marks in red paint on the sheep's backs—but it can be done. If you choose to wait impatiently, however, then you will suffer and the shepherd will suffer, and still the sheep will have to be guided across the road safely.

I was on my way to get my hair cut by my Muslim German friend at her 'ladies only' shop, where women can freely unveil inside, when my perfectly timed route suddenly faced the chaos of city sheep and goat herding. Once safely at my destination, sitting high on a chair in front of a mirror and being analysed in several different languages with regard to what could possibly be done about my burgeoning grey hairs, I realised I was fighting a battle against the grain of my nature. I actually like my grey hairs. I feel I've earned every single one of them and may even be able to name the specific event that spurred each of them on, so I can hardly be persuaded to pretend they don't exist. To me they are a sign of survival and acceptance—both miraculous accomplishments, worth celebrating. If I had too many at too young an age, I'm sure that would be a different story. If they suddenly jumped out at me in a hideous sort of way, I'd have to reconsider things. Having reached my 40s, though, I think I am entitled to a few eccentric luxuries of opinion.

Is there any relationship between liking my grey hairs and realising, shockingly, that I now think my fat deposits suit me just fine? This is not what I was raised by society to think but it was how I was designed by a Creator, who said 'very good'

41

when I was popped off the assembly line. My husband agrees, and so does my friend in our church's musical ensemble. She says she likes the way my extra arm skin waves when I try to direct the choir in short sleeves, because hers does, too. When I'm not completely consumed with my own 'self', with what I look like and how I appear to others, then I have all this free time on my hands. What to do with it?

Priorities of the heart: reevaluate them AOAP, As Often As Possible. What if I could channel my extra energy toward helping someone else? Where can I possibly fit in the circle of life here? Can I help the hungry, for example? That feels like a drop in the bucket, but still the bucket needs filling. Would it be enough today simply to embrace others in my heart, just as they were designed? Would waiting patiently for the sheep to pass count? How about deciding not to blast my non-BMW car past the rickety old donkey and his cart?

Affirming that God is good, true, faithful, present—that's a start. Maybe it will lead somewhere. Living fully in the present, enjoying God for ever: both of these things begin in the present. Paying attention, making conscious decisions, embracing life in all its rawness: each of these is a start for the heart in the right direction, and may even be a good finish, for today.

Whose rules?

One of my favourite images here
Is when country and city meet.
A herd of sheep and
taxi cabs—
whose rules will win in
the end?

To be happy

'What would it take for you to be happy?'
But I am happy now.
When I live in the present moment,
embracing, not fighting life.
Sweet and sour, dark and light,
pain mingled with joy,
laughter and tears—
all gifts to the soul,
ensuring depth and beauty.

'What would it take for you to be happy?'
Stay close to me now as ever.
Look at my heart, within, not without.
Water the garden you see.
Accept me just as I've been made,
although I'm different from you.
We can learn from each other's strengths
and move beyond our weaknesses.

'What would it take for you to be happy?'

But I am happy now.

9

Illegal: HIV/AIDS

Okorie's presence was already established when we appeared on the scene in Egypt. He was an in-residence Nigerian philosopher in addition to his duties as verger/custodian of St John's Church property. Whenever conflicts hit an impassable quandary, Okorie was present to offer his grounded advice. Usually his wise rulings appeared in the form of a simple solution, 'You just need to…', or a tangible image, 'My mouth was heavy, I could not tell you.' Every summer, when we returned from visiting family and friends, he would ask us, 'How are your people?' Each sentence he spoke was appended with 'You understand me?' With much laughter, shared tears and a transparent rapport, Okorie was a friend of my heart.

During our first few years in Cairo, Okorie was unmarried, and we rejoiced on the day he brought home his beautiful bride-to-be, Yetna. As he had no family here, my husband was asked to be the intermediary in the arrangement of this African marriage and began the dramatic process of asking for Yetna's hand from her father, who worked at Egypt's Nigerian Embassy. Their marriage was a memorable celebration and church members chipped in to make it a worthy event. From organising an African choir to arranging flowers, food and photography, all joined in the festivities. The image of Okorie appearing in a sharp Western suit and beaming with pride at his pointed crocodile shoes is a memory that still brings a smile.

Soon we welcomed their little son, Modupe, into our church

family, celebrating his baptism and his parents' desire to see him grow to love God. Modupe quickly developed from a good-natured baby into a toddler dashing about the church property, squealing with delight and mastering American 'high-fives'.

Then one day, out of the blue, life changed direction. Okorie was ill in bed for two weeks and his doctor told him he had hepatitis. I took his wife and son to our own Egyptian doctor to be inoculated, and was asked for Okorie's blood test results. I returned with the results the following day and was told I needed to rush Okorie in for an urgent examination. It was not hepatitis. Several experts later, shuttling back and forth from a diagnostic centre with a man who could barely stand, the results were inconclusive but immediate hospitalisation was required. It was advanced cancer, a tropical disease or perhaps HIV/AIDS.

Only three hospitals in the country could handle infectious diseases and we agreed to start at the top. Our youth director Erik and his taxi driver friend generously began a sleepless night monitoring progress (or lack of it) via telephone, while I drove Okorie's wife home. In spite of our doctor's insistence, the best-equipped hospital rejected him because of the fear that he was infected with AIDS and the 'no tolerance' rules of this country in relation to the disease. Even my husband must get a blood test before his work permit can be renewed each year. It is actually illegal to have HIV/AIDS in Egypt, so an infected foreigner is deported within 24 hours of the diagnosis.

In the early hours of the morning, Erik knocked on the doors of the second hospital and was told that they would not admit Okorie until a blood test showed proof that he did not have AIDS. This very poorly equipped facility asked Erik to take a vial of newly gathered blood to yet another lab. Even the taxi driver donned surgical gloves while Erik carried in his hand an unsealed vial of Okorie's blood during a bumpy taxi ride. Upon arrival at the lab, their request was refused as they were not family members. A battle of negotiations finally reached a truce and Okorie was allowed to spend the night at the hospital until the results could be sorted out the next morning. In the midst of dire conditions and the 'no tolerance' rules, the Egyptian hospital staff showed warm human care in their interactions with Okorie.

Sadly, the next day, two independent labs confirmed the same verdict: Okorie was in the final stage of AIDS. This meant being immediately ejected from hospital care and sent straight to the infamous 'fever hospital' to await deportation that night. Our doctor told us that he would refuse to send an animal there and heroically interceded yet again, so that Okorie was eventually released into our hands. His passport and address were officially recorded with the government security police until we could arrange a flight out of the country. As Okorie could no longer walk up the stairs to his apartment, he was sheltered at the church for his remaining hours in the country. He had weeks, perhaps months to live, if he could get good medical care back home.

We set Okorie up on a comfortable air mattress with a soft feather pillow and clean purple sheets. Friends arranged to stay with him around the clock and cater to his every request. Our doctor gave him several hours on an IV drip at his clinic to provide the nourishment he needed for the journey ahead.

Hundreds of Africans filed through the church property that day to say goodbye. Our Western expatriate church members and their families emerged by nightfall to sit in vigil with Okorie, Yetna and little Modupe. We reminisced with our favourite stories of times shared, laughed, passed around tissues for tears, and prayed together for God's sustaining strength. As we left that evening, our hearts overflowed with the knowledge of God's faithfulness, past, present and future.

Names have been changed.

I am thirsty

I am thirsty today,
yet not for a drink
but for
your river to flow.

I see and sense so many in need.
Please will
you
intercede?

I lift them toward your
heavenly throne.
I pray
your river will flow,
down through mountain passes
steep,
reaching the valleys
below.

Only you can quench
our thirst
and meet the needs of
your children.

10

Pets matter

After embarking on my Egyptian adventure and experiencing
scenes that mingled images of human poverty with packs of
underfed roaming street dogs, I now realise that pets are a
luxury for a life here. If you can manage it, though, loving
an animal makes sense because of the qualities that pets can
contribute to your life, such as endless cheerfulness and a
warm presence. It was tough going through the trauma of
permanently giving away our 'baby' shih-tzu to be pampered
in the US by neighbours while we ventured into the concrete
desert. We'd owned him for all four years of his life. Our pup
had been bred to sit on the laps of emperors, be professionally
groomed every month, eat a scientifically engineered diet and
patrol the greenest of backyard domains. He would not have
survived the uprooting.

As many expatriates do here, we experimented with the
whole range of pet options available. They all died off one
by one—rabbit, hamster and a slew of guinea pigs. After too
much grieving, we settled for enjoying the visit of wild birds to
our windowsill. The first 'regular' bird to appear was a Middle
Eastern feather-footed pigeon that we named Farruk. Although
his life expectancy in the wild would be only five years, six
years after our arrival he continues to peer in at our window,
cooing 'hello' every morning. Laughing doves, fancy pigeons
and house sparrows quickly discovered the fresh seed I placed
in an empty flowerbox attached to the windowsill.

Several years after we moved to Cairo, the offer of 'Pepsi' appeared. Pepsi was an eight-year-old, cola-coloured, lovable mutt with a limp from a mis-set broken bone that she'd suffered as a puppy. Kenya was her birth country but she had willingly participated in her owners' globe-hopping. Due to allergies in the family, she was kept as an outdoor dog, but now she would be unable to accompany them to their next posting, in Geneva. The company provided only a flat for accommodation, which would make Pepsi's outdoor life impossible. The family were almost resigned to putting her to sleep because no one wanted an old, tired dog, but then my daughter Britelle heard about her at school from a friend. Our only 'rules' for a possible future pet were that it should be housebroken, small and not prone to shedding hair. Well, she is housebroken...

You've heard it said that owners sometimes look like their dogs? I certainly feel how Pepsi looks some days—a happy demeanour but nevertheless limping along. If I trip up (*when* I trip up), I need traction and excessive doses of tender loving care. She makes me feel that life isn't as bad as it looks some days—but then, if I slept all day, like she does, I might be eternally peaceful, too.

Actually, Pepsi is the perfect creature for our home, and she picks up the slack for the family where my mothering fails. She exudes ideals that I cannot sustain—unconditional love, optimism, cheerfulness—and she never, ever holds a grudge. Her presence is a gift to our lives. Ever faithful and trusting, she sweeps along, creating a trail of warm love.

The birds on my windowsill have continued to bring me a deep but simple joy. Although the fruit trees in the area could probably provide all the food they need, caring for them with the small gesture of seed has brought me a return of great happiness.

A dove

A dove waited
patiently
upon my windowsill.

Perhaps I hadn't realised
but the seed I'd left out was gone.

Surely she didn't need
my help.
Fruit trees could provide seed for her young.
But she'd been told,
by God or by instinct,
to let me join in her care.
A dove, a symbol for
peace and God's Spirit;
heaven has opened again.

11

Avoiding prayer ruts—and a glimpse of a holy moment

The Islamic holy month of Ramadan had just begun and it was a perfect occasion to talk about prayer with our youngest church school members. Had anyone ever seen someone praying outside? Why did they think the people bowed down and touched their heads to the ground? Had anyone ever been to Jerusalem? Had they seen the old temple wall and people putting pieces of paper into its stone cracks? Why did we sometimes fold our hands to pray? Why did we often close our eyes? We had successfully explored the Lord's Prayer and clarified the usual confusion about 'hallowed' and 'trespasses', and they were going to say the prayer again when they rejoined their parents during Holy Communion. Next we moved on to prayer in our hearts, how we had prayers to say 'thank you' and also prayers that made our hearts feel a little bit heavy.

Our craft activity was to decorate a 'prayer box' with a slit in the top and then squeeze in our 'heart prayers'—one happy, one more serious—written or drawn on paper. The youngest boy drew himself as a stick figure with coathanger-shaped arms folded reverently. Some kept asking for more pieces of coloured paper on which to write new prayers springing to mind moment by moment. Others put in their two prayers and just smiled peacefully. No one explained to them the idea of putting a prayer in a box so that they could let go of their worries or make the 'thank you' more tangible, but they knew it intuitively: they are too young to have fallen into prayer ruts. Nothing has derailed their channels of communication with God yet.

Some children chose to show everyone their finished prayers before the papers disappeared into the box, but most didn't. The prayers that were enthusiastically verbalised usually had to do with a sick friend or a family member. 'Thank you' prayers were very popular. Some prayers quickly became dramatic— for example, mentioning a crime that had been committed, and including prayers for the criminal as well as the victim. Then they moved on to prayers about pets, and then animals in general. I could picture Jesus gathering the little children to himself and enjoying their chatter. No wonder he used the analogy that we must become like little children in order to enter the kingdom of heaven (Matthew 18:3). I really felt I should suggest that they preached the next sermon. They were in tune without trying, living the essence of prayer.

As I wondered at the beauty of what I experienced with the children that day, I was reminded of another image of prayer I had seen just outside the walls of our churchyard. I had been walking back from church as the sun beat high in the sky. Passing a deserted corner plot, I noticed how it reeked horribly of rubbish, roasting in the heat. As I glanced toward the offending source, I noticed a rubbish collector bending down to carefully arrange a rescued piece of clean cardboard. The Islamic call to prayer of the *muezzin* was echoing in the distance. In response, the old man knelt and bowed faithfully and reverently until his forehead touched the ground, humbling himself before God.

In stumbling across this scene, I felt I had glimpsed a holy moment: a spot that, at my first glance, was a place of rotting rubbish had been transformed into a place of prayer.

The road I walk

Would Jesus walk the road I walk
If he trod earth again?

I thought I saw his face today,
but it was an old
Muslim man.
He'd spread his cardboard on the ground
and bowed to say a
prayer.
Perhaps what I saw was insincere?
Would God even hear his
words?

But as I passed by silently,
I knew
my Lord was there.

12

HMPs versus VIPs

The distinction between HMPs (High Maintenance People) and VIPs (Very Important People) is really a bit absurd in itself. Of course we all fall into the category of VIPs as recipients of divine approval by our Creator. However, the ebb and flow of High Maintenance People in and out of our lives is a reality that we have to face.

Maybe I am wrong in thinking that the wife of an international church minister in Egypt is the only person in the world having to deal with such 'opportunities', but I doubt it—and I suppose it wouldn't be very shocking to discover that a few of us are actually HMPs for someone else. Banish the thought!

If you have a personality like my husband's—assertive, extraverted but sensitive—you probably have naturally built-in mechanisms to ward off the manipulative techniques of others. However, if you fall into another category—non-assertive, people-pleasing and a good listener, like me, for example—then you will know that managing all your admirers is a necessity. Some days it may feel like a juggling act and other days like walking a tightrope. The key is to stay centred; don't lose your balance.

Believe it or not, if you crash in emotional exhaustion and melt down on a regular basis, you are not being helpful either to yourself or to your needy HMPs. If you continually respond to their every whim, they will not diversify and will keep all their crises firing full blast in your direction.

Identifying your HMPs' issues and needs is crucial. For one, you cannot meet needs that only God can meet, such as the need for constant companionship or a listening ear for every complaint. It just isn't going to happen. Have you ever put unrealistic expectations on someone you love? I'm sure you haven't—but on the off-chance that you have, you will know it's not a good idea. So write a list of all your HMPs and then try to figure out what the first person on your list is looking for. You may be surprised to find that their goals are not to have on-call free counselling and to be your exclusive friend. If you're unlucky, those may be their exact intentions: at least you'll know what you are dealing with and can adjust accordingly.

Next, as you peruse your HMP list, you will need to set some boundaries for yourself, such as respecting your days off as exactly that—days off. Don't rush to the rescue of your HMP unless it is a genuine emergency. Often, an empathetic moment on the telephone is enough. Maintain a balanced, healthy lifestyle so that you have some margin in your emotional life for real emergencies.

Ensure that you are fed internally before reaching out to meet the needs of others. That may mean planning some time into your weekly schedule specifically for things that nurture you. For me, those might include a bit of quiet reflection, reading, exercise, playing music, journal writing, an evening of fun family interaction and, as often as possible, a weekly lunch date with my husband. If you do not consciously express your own boundaries, you are doomed to drown in a dry desert. Trust me—it's possible, and you really don't want to go there. Even when you tell yourself that you will only see so-and-so once a week or even less often, it will take a few tries to get it right. You parents—do you remember weaning your baby? Well, it's a process, just like that. At this point you are not juggling or walking a tightrope but riding a see-saw.

One of the rules of the game is never to do harm; that includes to yourself, as well as to others. I think there is only one dear HMP/VIP in my whole church who doesn't like the music I choose each week. The only time she remembers to point out her useful suggestions to me is immediately following every service—very effective. Whenever I invite her to tea at my home, she never thinks to mention the matter. If only I could remember the wisdom of Okorie, our Nigerian former philosopher/grounds-keeper who used to tell me so simply, 'You have to learn that you cannot please everyone.' It took me a while to work out my own methodical plan of defence in this particular situation, but what made the difference was explaining my tactics to my family—to avoid my musical expert friend after church at all costs. I slipped up the other week and my son came over ever so politely to interrupt our conversation, asking to be driven home. Bless him.

Another tool in my defensive arsenal is the telephone answering machine; we don't have caller ID in Egypt yet. There are certain times of day when I won't answer the phone unless I am fully prepared to talk to the person who happens to be at the very top of my HMP list. It is amazing how many of their emergencies resolve themselves without my services.

Please don't get me wrong. It is not that I am unwilling to help people or uninterested in their concerns. It's just that I've learnt the hard way what happens when my list is at full capacity. Where is the time, then, for all the other people who make up our little Cairo parish? There are friends I love to spend time with from our church book club, and we receive many invitations to share meals with members of our congregation or local community. They are not demanding, yet they are still important. Also, I have discovered that I am more sincere, more loving, more helpful and true when I am emotionally running on full rather than empty.

We are all fellow pilgrims stumbling along in muck some days and flying on the wings of the wind other days. What a gift life is in all its colours—dark as well as light! How wonderful that our Creator does not categorise us with personality acronyms; how wonderful that his list is never full. I love reading about Jesus' first disciples. Talk about high maintenance! No wonder Jesus soaked in the silence of the Middle Eastern hills and rested in prayer in God's presence. Now we have the gift of God's breath, his very Spirit, to guide us when we are listening to him and to one another. May we never forget that each of us was created to be a delight, to bear the image of the divine. May we have eyes that see and ears that hear the mysteries within ourselves and within each another.

Inside the heart

Seeking to shape souls to be
just like your own—
how do you know that's the plan?

Can't we just trust the work of
our Master
whose spirit formed each one?
To see inside the heart of another,
you must look past the external.
Then inside you'd recognise
a soul just as your own.

How do we see from out to in?
Not with ordinary eyes.

But God will freely give the gift,
if you so desire.

the heart

Living water

Grant me
living water,
Lord.
My well dries up
so quickly.

Living

13

The day my daughter fell into a hole

I have already mentioned Mokkattam, nestled into the edge of Cairo, not far from the vast Citadel Fortress, where our friends the *zebellin* (rubbish collectors) live. The Citadel, one of the highest points of elevation in Cairo, was originally founded in AD1176 by the famed Muslim commander Saladin. Its mosques, museums and battlements reflect a diverse heritage. Shadowed by its imposing image is the dusty winding road to Mokkattam.

Now some 30,000 strong, this community, culturally Christian, was the only place my family visited, before moving to Egypt, that drew us back two days in a row. Why, in the burning summer heat, we would want to experience its potent odours and the heart-wrenching squalor of its inhabitants' living conditions can be explained only in mystical terms.

My children had shared our interest in visiting the famous cave church, built on the site where St Simon the Tanner had reportedly moved a mountain in the tenth century. Being very interested in religious dialogue, the Muslim Caliph at that time had invited the Coptic Pope and a prominent Jewish leader for a visit. One thing led to another and something like Elijah's Mount Carmel confrontation (1 Kings 18) was proposed. The Caliph had been hoping for a reason to demolish the imposing Mokkattam hill, which blocked his view toward the east. The Pope was asked to prove that his religion was 'true' by doing what Christ had said was possible: 'with faith as small as a mustard seed you can move a mountain' (see Matthew 17:20). If the Pope proved unable to facilitate such a miracle, it would lead to the demise of his people: the Caliph would give Coptic Christians the choice to leave Egypt altogether or be executed.

The word got out and, after three days of prayer and fasting by Christians throughout Egypt, the Pope was led to choose St Simon as the mediator in this project to move Mokkattam mountain. On the set day, many people gathered, pleading *Kyrie eleison* ('Lord, have mercy'). In the words of Iris El-Masri, author of *The Story of the Coptic Church* (Middle East Council of Churches, 1975), 'The mountain was thrusting up and down, and the sun could be seen from under it.' The Caliph, shaking with fear, embraced the Pope warmly and this marked the beginning of a long friendship between the two. Simon humbly faded from the scene and could not be found to share in the ensuing festivities.

The cave church that we went to visit was founded just 30 years ago, during a construction project, when a huge rock disappeared into a hole. The discovery of this hole soon led to the digging out of a large cave to form a church, which solved the growing need for a place of worship for the community, thanks to the lifelong dedication of a local Coptic priest and many others over the years. Today a larger amphitheatre has been dug out of the mountain, where you can find 9000 people worshipping God together every Thursday evening (the beginning of the Islamic weekend). A Polish artist has sculpted stunning biblical scenes into the limestone hills surrounding the area for the benefit of its illiterate occupants. This spectacular effort has brought otherwise inaccessible stories to life. Often I've pondered the significance of these images called to mind by the story of the cave church—holes, caves, darkness, then light.

One year, one month, one week, one day, my daughter fell into a hole here in Egypt. It was not a literal hole but a pit of despair and darkness. We'd been walking together along the path of life for 13 years by then. All of a sudden, without any warning, she fell straight into this hole.

At first she was not swallowed completely but she was sinking faster and faster. I had no idea how deep the hole was; she began to slide out of sight. I called to her. I ran for help. I threw her a rope through my tears; I shouted words of encouragement—but she could not grab hold of the rope.

For many days and weeks and months, I watched as she slipped further down. I myself could not get her out. Our only hope would be her Creator, calling to her heart with tender, loving words that only she could hear.

More than once I had told her the tale of holes that I'd fallen into over the years. Help often did not appear until I felt I'd hit the bottom. But knowing and experiencing are two different things. My daughter would have to discover on her own the strength and presence that would be sufficient to carry her through anything.

I wrestled with nightmares and agonised with memories day and night. Had I perhaps pushed her in? No, no, she had simply fallen. Yet still I agonised. Why could I not pull her out? Why wouldn't she grab on to the rope?

Time spiralled on: I found myself remembering my own dark times again—and that brought a sudden flood of hope. I recalled the warmth of strong arms at the bottom of my own pit. My Creator never explained what was happening; it was a mystery, but I found his presence sustaining me within. When my ears became deaf and my eyes were blind, a divine Guide carried me through. People had thrown ropes—I needed them—but first, strength had to well up from deep inside, from the depths of my soul. Some days I could sense God's whisper; some days I could feel the strength that held me. It sustained me and told my heart truth.

Then one day my hole became cold; I was forced to search around. Soon I discovered a ray of light, shining down from above. Only a glimpse of a tiny shaft could be seen but it was enough to illuminate the rope that others had thrown to me. So tired was I that to grasp it was impossible. Instead, unseen hands pushed me higher, towards the growing light. Eventually I tumbled out into the fresh air. Sunshine smiled on me with a breeze of welcome. I was free.

Now here I stand, staring down at my daughter. She's fallen into a hole; I've thrown her a rope. I've planned her 'welcome home' party. I remind myself of God's goodness, his offer of strength sufficient for all we face. It's truth. It's joy. It's life. I remind myself because she can't hear my voice yet. May she find those warm arms sustaining her.

She did.

Entrusted with a charge

I've been thinking about people I admire and why:
Jesus, Mother Teresa,
my husband, my parents,
my children, my neighbours
out in the streets of Cairo.

Purpose, sacrifice, trusting grace.
I long to follow their footsteps.

They make it look so effortless.
If only I could keep up!
But maybe I'm on this journey
for reasons yet unknown.
My fellow pilgrims span the centuries
of places, races, creeds.

Purpose, sacrifice, trusting grace.
On we persevere.

All a part of the human family:
image bearers of God.
No matter if our lights are small;
they still dispel the darkness.
We've been entrusted with a charge in life
which simply is to be.

'Be still and know that I am God.'
Live in mindfulness
now.

- *14* - *

Life-giving source

I have two Egyptian friends who live ten miles apart, in apartment buildings not very far from the Nile. They both love God and have dreams for their children; they both experience suffering and joy. One is the driver for our bishop here. The other has a staff of chauffeurs.

I love their spirits. Both are sincere, joyful and outwardly focused—and yet, when they return home each night, a million miles divide them. One is welcomed home by the skills of a butler, the other by a tired wife. One sits down to a meal cooked by servants. The other lives with no kitchen; instead his wife works on a makeshift range. He says that in the last 20 years she has never complained. Please, please don't ask my husband— I couldn't promise the same.

The eldest child of one is in England at a prestigious university, while her younger children attend school with my own. The eldest child of the other friend is dependent, mentally disabled since birth. Thankfully, his two younger children have had an education, with caring supporters even seeing them through college. Perhaps they hope the cycle of poverty will end.

It is humbling to think of the paths chosen for us even as life begins. My heart has learnt so much from my friends— how much they give to others despite their very different circumstances, one so privileged, the other so vulnerable. Jesus' story of the widow's mite is alive and well (Luke

21:1–4). This is one of my favourite stories in the Bible. Jesus reveals to us a glimpse of his character: he looks at the heart, not the outward actions of those giving to the temple treasury. Similarly I think of my two friends here—the contrast between the poor and the wealthy—but in this case I sense that both give of themselves from their hearts. Every time I am with them I feel tremendously encouraged.

My friend born to wealth is exceedingly generous, regularly providing food baskets for Christian refuge children here in Cairo. At the same time, the family employs hundreds of workers in its organic farming business and generously provides housing for them all, near the farm, as well as educating their children. My friend says we are not just children of Abraham but also of God, our Creator. She vocalises her sense of God's Spirit across religious boundaries, which warms me to her.

Although material resources are dramatically less available to my other friend, he is continually giving of himself. He calls my husband regularly to see how our family is doing. Sometimes, after our weekly church service, he will proudly present his family to say 'thank you' for the ways we have been able to assist them. Yet their smiles and generous handclasps return to us far more than we could ever give.

My two friends live miles apart, yet they are linked as human beings and linked with me. God bridges our hearts through friendship and prayers, and by teaching us to offer practical love to whomever appears in our lives each day. Our only audience is God, who looks at our hearts with great love.

In the same way that my two friends give life to my heart, despite the desert times that I experience, so the ancient life-giving river, the Nile, stretches through this barren land of Egypt. Along its shores dwell well-watered lives, dependent on its source. If it disappeared, so much green vegetation would immediately turn into desolate desert. If you fly along the length of Egypt's section of the Nile, the dependency of the people on this water is extremely evident. For several miles on either side, the earth is well nourished, and then the desert encroaches with a dramatic break from vibrant green to barren brown. Our section of the river in Cairo is polluted with rubbish and disease, but the further south you go, the clearer it becomes until it meets up with the great dam in Aswan.

Moses was rescued along the Nile's banks (Exodus 2:3–9), probably in answer to his mother's heartfelt prayers. There is an old synagogue just a few miles from where we live that marks the spot where Jews believe that Moses was pulled from the reeds along the edge of the river. A large marble sarcophagus apparently houses the original papyrus basket. I asked once if I could look inside but was only smiled at, kindly, and ignored. As refugees, Jesus and his parents crossed over this river into safety. Our district of Cairo, *Maadi*, means 'the crossing', in memory of the holy family's passage across the Nile to safety during their flight to Egypt from Herod's threats. Our home is just a mile from where a large Coptic church marks their life-saving crossing.

For centuries, the Nile has had a symbolic significance, like other great rivers around the world. These mighty waterways capture the imagination, nourishing humanity literally and symbolically. On an island in the middle of the Nile in Cairo stands an ancient 'Nile-o-meter'. Water marks in a large stone cistern would indicate the potential health of Egyptian crops for the year to come. The pharaohs, to help predict the coming flood season, visited it annually and made lavish gifts to its guardian.

Living as a young girl in Central Africa, I remember riding on a boat down the Nile. My memories are of muddy water, yet a happy home to hippos and crocodiles. When I saw the source of the Nile, Lake Victoria, I never dreamed that the adventure of life would lead me to the other end of its length.

Each week in church, we sing a setting of the *Gloria* at the beginning of our worship service. It's an arrangement assembled from a third-century Egyptian *Gloria*, which I put to an old Hebrew tune that sings in praise of creation, with the Great River, the Nile, representing our life-giving Source. The Great River symbolises strength and refreshment for me in a way that the barren wilderness does not (although, when I set eyes on the beauty of the rolling sand sea of the Sahara near the Libyan border one year, I could understand the gift of the desert as well). Our Egyptian *Gloria* includes allusions to snorkelling in the Red Sea, and observing the awesome colours of coral and fish below. One month I introduced a new *Gloria* to the congregation to add variety, but was soon persuaded to return to our weekly reminder of God's blessing here in Egypt, linking us back to the third century and beyond.

May none of God's works keep silence,
night or morning.
Bright stars, Great River, the depth of the seas,
expanse of the open desert.
May all break into song, to Father, Son and Spirit.
May all heaven join in.
Amen. Amen. Amen.
Power, grace, honour and glory
to God the giver of life.
Amen. Amen. Amen.

SOURCE UNKNOWN

Our Great River

Who would have thought to put a
river
amid a desert land?
Our source of
life
has cared for us
and fed us without end.

The life-giving strength of our
Great River—
a source I often ponder.
Moses was drawn from these very shores.
and God used him to set his people
free.

River

Jesus the refugee

This land sheltered Jesus, a
refugee,
one in a line of many.
Lives in dire need
sustained
by generous care ingrained.

refugee

- 15 -

Dangers

Although my request for life insurance was denied because I live in Egypt—'near a war zone', as they worded it—safety is, surprisingly, a minimal concern for us. Of course we have been affected by bombings of one sort or another during our years here, but, as they are seldom and random, it is not an obsession for us. Thankfully, personal friends of ours who have been at the scene of such horrible ravages have survived, but the emotional toll of such encounters has had lasting effects on many. Our hearts have ached for those innocent lives, destroyed in vain acts of violence.

The Egyptian government is strongly opposed to all such selfish expressions of desperation. The worldwide spiritual head of Sunni Islam is based here at the historic Al-Azhar Mosque, and he speaks out against the killing, too.

I have had more than one moment of wondering 'What if?' as I've dropped my children off at their international American school on a high-alert day. Bomb squad dogs are not just standing by but are actively investigating each of our vehicles. One especially tense morning, I dropped my son off at school and, within minutes of returning home, heard an explosion in the distance. I desperately called Paul-Gordon, in a state beyond complete panic, to find out what was happening. It turned out to be a dynamite blast in a quarry just out of town.

At times, the US embassy will send out warnings of organised demonstrations and encourage us to steer clear of central

Cairo. Such events are better planned and controlled than spontaneous acts of violence. Often on Fridays, the weekly day of prayer, our local police station deploys soldiers in riot gear in case some propaganda machine or other, trying to infiltrate our peaceful society, has generated a hostile sermon. Our church has generously been provided with round-the-clock armed guards; my husband knows all their names. He treats them as friends, and the mutual respect is obvious as they see him arrive and offer their enthusiastic greetings.

Just an hour before our church service one Saturday evening, a suicide bomber jumped from a bridge near the museum, down at Tahrir Square in the centre of town. One of our Egyptian friends immediately ran over to make sure Paul-Gordon was not at the diocese headquarters nearby. Church felt a bit more bonding that day. During Holy Communion, the US Regional Security Officer in our congregation was informed of a second attack by the suicide bomber's sister and fiancée on a tourist bus at the edge of town, at the Citadel. We were directed to proceed home immediately following the service. The recessional hymn that day was 'Be thou my vision', its words reminding me of our need for God's care and presence throughout our earthly pilgrimage. We all left the church building to discover a swarm of Egyptian police, bravely surrounding our church walls to protect us until more was known of the rampage underway.

Ironically, we usually feel safer here than we do on visits to the US these days. We never have to worry about child abduction or molestation. Family values run deep and we see the love of children played out in front of us daily. Especially when our children were younger, they would be stopped in public settings, admired, and usually given a sweet treat before being sent on their way. Our teenagers happily get themselves around Cairo in taxis, on foot, or down the Nile on hired feluccas. Before we moved to Egypt, many people commented on the element of danger in moving a family to the Middle East. I remember one woman in my Bible study, soon after 9/11, saying, 'I hate Arabs.' I was a bit surprised at her bluntness and asked if she had any Arab friends. No—she had never met one.

The warm local welcome we received in Cairo has surprised many Americans with whom we've stayed in contact. One summer, while we were visiting our church in the US, a friend took me aside and pleaded with me to return to the US for the sake of our children. It was an eye-opener for her to be told that we wanted to stay overseas for exactly that reason—for the sake of our children—and more. Their worldviews have expanded enormously through their experiences here and their friends represent a whole world of religions and cultures. First-hand friendships move them far beyond the vocabulary of religious dialogue or tolerance. Our daughter's last birthday party included ten friends—Muslim, Christian, Hindu and agnostic—from Egypt, Lebanon, Italy, Chile, India, Puerto Rico, the UK, America and Korea.

Without question, the only real danger the children face is traffic. Imagine you are playing an arcade driving game. Add a big city setting and piles of cars, and take away the rules. There are no traffic signals to heed, a few useless roundabouts to ignore, and taxis, minibuses, donkeys and bodies to dodge at every turn. This daily danger is real and unavoidable.

Aware of life

Mindfulness—
aware of
life
in the present moment.

Gratefulness—
celebrating,
looking and living
deeply.

Aware

Trash bin files

My 'trash bin files' first appeared in the form of a clandestine notebook, which I designated 'journal overflow'. I sometimes imagined it as being in the genre of ancient archaeological jottings, if such things ever existed, purposely undelivered into the hands of a scribe. This notebook would *not* be the sort of document that I'd lock in a safety deposit box with instructions to be read upon my demise; quite the opposite. If my house caught fire, it would be the only thing I'd be relieved to see go up in flames. These files were to be deleted and destroyed at regular intervals; they were certainly never to fall into the hands of another human being. Only God could handle the necessary emotional venting that took place in them, and I myself shook in dismay when reading back some of the entries. Pages cried, screamed, threw tantrums, begged, bribed and gave up hope. All were heartfelt prayers from the darkest side of me—layer upon layer to be sorted, filed and eventually thrown away. Yet, thankfully, the act of writing did save me from verbally spewing all those thoughts that I really didn't want to claim anyway. I know how tiring it is to be on the receiving end of constant complaints so I certainly didn't want to spread more around.

Of course, this doesn't mean that my regular journal is a field of happy sunflowers. It, too, is raw and honest but it explores faith issues and processes experiences that I know, on future readings, I'll be pleased to see I've survived. It has the potential to record progress and growth—one lunge forward, two steps backward, with lots of celebrating in between, a bit like a game of Snakes and Ladders. My trash bin files, on the other hand, were all about the 'snakes', slipping down into emotional oblivion and hoping I wouldn't be completely destroyed when I hit the bottom. Maybe an old feather mattress would be waiting—or possibly a trampoline, to rocket me out of the well of despair altogether?

Expressing my pain in that worn spiral notebook of trash bin files was like draining fluid from a swollen injury. At least the poison of negativity was laid bare, and God's surgery was imminent.

To put it another way, it was like house-cleaning. At a snail's pace I started to dig in my drawers full of junk and then moved on to sweeping out obscure corners of my soul, dark as unexplored pyramid chambers. Once the issues were visible and committed to the realm of conscious thought, the Spirit's light could shine on them and offer a respite.

I didn't reread the files all the time; it wasn't as if I couldn't bear to let go of pain. But I knew they were there when all else failed—and I knew I would trash the evidence as soon as I was ready. When that day arrived, whenever I felt ready to destroy the pages assembled so far, there was always something very rewarding and sustaining about it. Ripping up trash bin files is a tangible healing ceremony. All the witnesses are present—your heart, your thoughts, your spirit, your mind, your emotions, and God. The life-threatening grip of negativity is broken and the emotional scars fade over time. The words on those pages proved I was human, for better or for worse. They made me honest with myself and before God.

As you can imagine, my husband was well aware of the impact of the emotions that were not processed smoothly through my trash bin files. I know it was a very confusing time for him, to see his normally cheerful wife so down-hearted. We both realised that the uprooting of our family was a risk on many levels but we had no idea of the dark roads we would meet on our journey—although we were thankful that the children had, on the whole, settled well. There really wasn't much he could do besides being patient and present, until God's Spirit guided us through. I would never want to experience such emotional turmoil again, but we bonded together over time and are closer today than we could ever have been if we had experienced only clear skies and smooth roads.

Emotions don't call for judgment but sometimes they are windows into unclear thinking. They are what they are: they are there to feel and to process and to move through. The Source of goodness and strength walks the trail of life with us, for ever present, whether we understand completely or not.

Creating and destroying trash bin files proves that you're in motion, gleaning little truths along the way to celebrate and pass on to others. Above all, if you are going through such turmoil, never panic if you find the trash bin files overflowing. The sun will shine again. You will walk in freedom; you will soar in truth. Allow yourself to be who you were designed to be. Don't reject God's gift of yourself, created in light to live life, embrace suffering and give joy to your Maker.

Out of control

My world is spinning out of control.
When will rest rescue me?

Sometimes I wonder if the crushing walls
will succeed in doing me in.

I dream of a place where quiet reigns,
where nature generously restores.

If such a place exists on earth,
then hope will not flicker out.

I am yours, my Master, my Friend.
I seek to honour your name.

Remind me of your strength today,
your power to calm the storm.

control

Having to stop

Today my husband's name is Hope.
I'd hate to be in his shoes—

having to stop along the race
to try to understand

why his partner can't take one more step
and needs to rest again.

Today he shows me patience and love,
he leans down to take my hand.

He decides to let us rest awhile.
We discover quiet waters.

And fields we had been running past
are pastures full of green.

Having to

– 17 –

One morning in the life
of a summer respite

Often, the clarity of what I experience in Cairo is most in focus when I am off the spinning wheel of chaos and soaking in my annual summer respite. During the hot summer months in Egypt, an annual mass exodus occurs. Expatriates return to their home countries and Egyptians who can afford to leave do so, often migrating temporarily to the Mediterranean coast to stay cool. Our family has been blessed to return to a small flat near a forest reserve in the US each summer for a time of much-needed renewal.

The first thing I notice each year on our return is the ringing of my ears in the quietness. This experience continues for several days as I marvel at the sound of silence—audible, almost tangible after ten months of high-decibel noise, day and night.

Morning is announced by the happy chatter of birds outside my window. I smile and relax as I realise I have been treated to a full night's sleep without an air purifier drowning out car alarms, train horns and the voices of security guards beneath my bedroom window. Instead, the calling of cardinals and the knocking of woodpeckers welcome me to the day. I stretch my jetlagged body and look forward to a walk in the still, quiet hours of dawn. I have had a full year of indoor exercise, without the opportunity to escape outside each time I desperately need to clear my head or breathe fresh air. Within the first week back, my pollution-induced asthma will subside and my throat and chest will relax. I grab the first pair of shorts I've worn since the previous summer and skip out to greet the geese waddling by. No growling packs of wild street dogs on the prowl. The sky is pure cobalt blue. No smog. Not even a cloud in sight.

As it is every year, one of the most dramatic readjustments to life soaked in nature involves the retraining of my breathing. No more inhaling through my mouth to avoid the smell of car exhaust and rotten rubbish. Clover from prairie fields wafts its fragrance my way. I gulp it in and savour each breath. Defenses loosen; renewal begins. In the distance I hear church bells ringing, replacing the mosque calls that usually remind me to pray. But I am praying already, thankfulness welling up from deep within.

Back at the entrance to our flat, I notice that my shoes are not dusty. I barely register the lack of buzzing activity to welcome me home: no guards staring, no building attendants waving in greeting, just a securely locked door. I think of the 'safety' conversation that Paul-Gordon and I have every summer, which we rarely discuss in Cairo. How far can our children ride their bikes away from home? Alone? Together? Is the forest off limits again this year? I unlock the door and find my two teenagers already surfing a high-speed Internet and flipping through hundreds of English-language television channels with no worries that power cuts will interrupt their activities. I take a deep drink straight from the tap. No need to call the local market to have bottled water delivered. Actually, I doubt that any grocer in town would agree to such a request here, anyway.

Eager to play my concert harp again, I remove its blue velvet storage cover and marvel again at the lack of dust. Its strings have been loosened for the year to take pressure off the soundboard, so it will take days of tuning and replacing atrophied strings before I can play regularly—not to mention the ground I've lost in technique and agility.

Next on the morning's agenda is a trip to the grocery shop. I won't need to cook everything from scratch tonight. As I get into the car, I remind myself that rules of the road do exist: stay in one lane, keep to the speed limit, stop at traffic signals and don't honk rudely. Surprisingly, a car waits patiently as I back out of my driveway, and another driver waves me ahead with a smile. Where are the bumps? The roads are so wide. No rubbish is blowing around on the edges. So much space divides the houses along my route. Does only one family live in that building?

Once at the shop, I am immediately mesmerised by the fruit and vegetable section. Every piece is perfectly presented—no bruises, all washed clean, lettuce sanitary and ready to consume. Is it real? The fresh eggs don't have signs of chicken coops on them. Do I like the lack of earthy rawness? I watch a few other shoppers speed by while talking to non-present people on mobile phone headsets. It looks odd. No one is staring at me; I blend into my surroundings. If someone catches my eye, they smile. The queues to check out and pay for my groceries are straight. My cashier asks politely why I am gazing blankly at the machine to swipe my bank card. He lights up with enthusiasm when I explain I am just back from Cairo.

Soon I am back home, and no one rushes to my car to help carry my bags. The church bells ring again in the distance. I am home—or am I? This magical rediscovery continues throughout my summer respite. I live each day in the present, rarely finding my mind consciously wandering toward the Middle East until I see a veiled woman or get into an interesting political discussion. Every summer I reserve the final week for silence. Reconnection with friends and extended family is complete. It is time to refocus on the next year that awaits me in Cairo. I visit the prairie fields, search harder for deer in the fields and savour each blackberry I pick from its bush. By the last day I'am ready, and for several weeks after returning to Egypt I feel strong. Then my inner resolve starts to waver and I slowly begin the process of living from within once again. Six summers behind me. One day at a time to go.

A famine of nature and beauty

I wonder how long my soul can survive
a famine of nature and beauty.

My determined outward demeanour
is strong,
but quietly I cry from within.

Sometimes even I don't hear
or recognise my own plea.

I accept my current
boundaries,

yet long to thrive in
freedom.

Hardships

We share and bear each other's
burdens.
How lonely it would be,
if hardship never opened our door
and gave us reason to
need.

Hardships

- *18* -

The holy mundane: the story of Cairo grocery shopping

It was almost certain that the Carrefour supermarket would be teeming with shoppers today if I didn't get there when its doors opened. The last thing I needed was one more ounce of stress added to the weekly endeavour. The local markets are my '8-till-lates' but for planned menus I need efficiency. My watch is set by the expedition to gather food for the family, an adventure that many of my friends refuse to attempt behind the steering wheels of their own cars.

Today I gauged the traffic to be about typical, beeping and dodging and racing along as people dashed across the motorway, oblivious to the face of fate. I slowed down at the machine gun lookout post and stared down the barrel of a gun. The officer was lazily resting his chin on its length; no high-alert commands for today. Our police state is still recovering from the month of Ramadan's day-time fasting and night-time feasting. One of my fasting friends told me to imagine celebrating Christmas every night for 30 nights in a row. Wow!

I know this route well by now, after years of navigating the same bumps and holes—well, maybe they get a bit deeper and wider over time. A coughing car, engine spitting black smoke, ploughed in front of me, missing my front bumper by inches, which was enough. I held my breath and accelerated past two paint-peeling pick-up trucks, carefully loaded to the sky with people, black bags and worn-out office furniture. Next came a donkey cart, limping towards me down the wrong side of the road—trusting, faithful creature. Within minutes I could see the supermarket ahead but it would take skill to manoeuvre over in time to turn off. Past one lorry in the middle lane, now merged between two racing taxis, all I needed were three more seconds; I was forced to forfeit the win. I hate it when my lane disappears.

I pulled up to the makeshift bomb-check station at the entrance of the car park. It was 10.45am and the three guards on shift were either dead or fast asleep, dramatically slouched against each other on the waiting bench, automatic weapons sprawled. I slowed to a stop, saw their chests rising and falling and moved on; clearly they weren't on high alert, either.

The key to parking in the monstrous Carrefour car park is to slide in right next to a designated shopping trolley return area. Of course, the first section of the car park is always blocked off by the same crushed orange cones. This ensures that you have to exit by pushing your precariously functioning trolley past all the taxi drivers, lined up on the outside bench to enjoy the sight of you—I mean, to wait for their charges to fill their shopping baskets and return to be shuttled home. Last week was incredible, though: they were all gazing downward, meditating on their inspirational Ramadan reading. I love this month of reflection and renewal, and I always appreciate the year-round inspiration of seeing taxi drivers stopping for prayer, pulling out their clean rugs from inside their tired black-and-white cars and facing east as their foreheads touch the ground.

Today I walked by with purpose, got into the women's entrance line, had my bag checked twice for weapons, and claimed a trolley that still had four little wheels and a section for holding fragile items. Nothing unusual was happening today, although I noticed a new brand of orange juice imported from Saudi Arabia. It looked worth a try. Carrefour is a French (how can I put it?) super-Walmart-type store, which is owned here by the Saudis. They do funny promotions every once in a while in the aisles, but they seem to target the women who are covered head-to-toe in black and brush past me. Oh well, my survival Arabic would hardly hold up under grocery interview fire. After a Cairo shooting by a woman in full veil in May 2005, women are always watched with vigilance and can't even leave their trolleys in one aisle and walk to another. I'm still not sure why.

I was extremely happy to find some beautiful tomatoes today to pick through and admire. When they're good, they're very good. Cardamom-flavoured coffee was back. Paul-Gordon would be happy. No such luck with yogurt before its expiry date. Oh well, the children would be flexible. I got to the bottom of my shopping list and raced to the finish line. If I timed things right, I would be home in 23 minutes and our apartment block *boab* (security/building manager), Abdu, would be waiting to help me carry things in and recycle my valuable plastic bags.

On the way home, if you know where to look and the air pollution is not too bad, you can see the Great Pyramids of Giza in the distance. That's my favourite part of the drive. They dwarf the high-rises lining the Nile, which are much closer to me. No such luck today, though. Then a poem hit my brain—something to write on the run. I got back to the apartment 20 minutes later, tapping out syllables in my head, parked and pulled out my notepad. Bang, bang, bang: just Abdu knocking on my car window. He doesn't think a moment of silence is a good idea.

'Madame, Mr Paul gone to *kineesa* (church). Carrefour, heavy bags?'

'*Shoukran* (thank you), Abdu,' I smiled.

Another uneventful grocery shopping trip successfully completed… and a poem, 'My car in Cairo', is born.

My car in Cairo

I love to drive my car in Cairo—
it's like a video game.
Dodging buses, cars and bikes,
donkey carts and
sheep.
Pedestrians jostling for position.
Who will get the last
beep?

Adrenaline is pumping now.
One ways, roundabouts,
none of these suggested rules
apply to
us
today.
No traffic lights exist to hinder,
only
bumps and
holes.
The race is on and
time,
for once'
has meaning everywhere.

19

Ali Baba

Our life in Cairo is inescapably harmonised with the lives of our apartment block attendants, the *boabs*. Day and night their presence protects us from unsolicited guests; they pamper us with their help carrying heavy grocery bags, and rescue us repeatedly with regard to emergency repairs. Two brothers from Upper Egypt share this task in our building, resourcefully rotating their sleeping schedules and the visits of their families nearby. Always cheerful and gregariously attentive, the younger brother greets us with an unending supply of broad smiles as we leave and return home each day. More serious and responsible overall for our welfare, the older brother generously manages all our crises from sewage backups to empty gas bottles to electrical power box explosions.

A worn prayer rug graces the corner of our building's entryway, where the brothers take turns praying or often just sit pensively in repose from the assault of daily demands. After our own forages into the often-battering urban stimulus, to be received at home by such a calming scene is always welcome.

In addition to the very modest monthly fees that apartment owners and tenants supply, the *boabs* are dependent on commissioned errands to provide enough income to meet the needs of their families. Several years ago, when their shared mode of transportation, a bicycle, was officially pronounced irreparable, we readily volunteered to replace it, knowing how crucial a role it played in their lives. To us, this was a small financial outlay, but it was completely out of reach to them.

As is culturally appropriate, most of our dealings with the *boabs* take place through exchanges with my husband. My own daily encounters hover safely in the realm of polite greetings and grateful expressions. Now that our daughter is a teenager, these protective Arab brothers naturally scrutinise every one of her visitors, and questionable guests are announced in advance via intercom or personally escorted to our door for final approval. We were all completely horrified the day one of the brothers decided that one of our daughter's head-covered girlfriends should not be admitted. Apparently, his upbringing had taught him that Muslims and Christians were not friends, although it seemed a strange view to hold on to in modern-day Cairo. His defences gradually relaxed, though, as his own worldview began to broaden.

Life with our *boabs* usually hums along at a comfortably predictable pace. The rhythm of the annual month of fasting is certain to produce grumpy demeanours as blood sugar levels plunge, yet feast days present lavish contrasts of infectious enthusiasm. One autumn afternoon, I returned home and noticed that a dusty cloud of gloom had settled over the occupied prayer rug corner. The only other time I'd seen the cheerful brother depressed had been when their oldest brother was killed in a car crash. Our family dinner conversation that evening inevitably included the depressing atmosphere hovering in our building and the *boabs*' mysterious predicament. My husband quickly revealed the cause for such mourning: their bicycle had been ridden off from the local market by a thief.

The expression 'someone must have needed it more than they did' did not apply. Resigned to the ripple of consequences that the loss of their bicycle would incur, the brothers had not taken into account the possibility of a happy solution. Already that year, the younger brother, who wasn't afraid of dogs, had lost his freelance pet-walking job when he'd been unable to rescue his fluffy charge from the jaws of a pillaging street dog.

Now, just weeks away loomed the *Eid-al-Adha*, the annual Muslim celebration of Abraham's willingness to sacrifice his son and God's intervention in that important event. Typically, the build-up to the commemoration is palpable, with excited greetings and additional blessings added to daily exchanges. Pressure would be intense for our *boabs* to provide a lamb to sacrifice in symbolic remembrance—though a chicken would do, if finances were tight. It felt glaringly right for us to thwart the anonymous thief's act and fund yet another bicycle (and lock) immediately. It would preserve both brothers' family needs and ensure the continued trickling down of finances past their wives and children to the home of their beloved mother, far off in Upper Egypt.

As expected, our *boabs* were visibly relieved when, the following morning, we assured them that we would buy them a new bicycle. That same evening, they unveiled their brand new bike with great pride and thanks. A large blue basket was attached to the front for carrying groceries, and two impressive chain locks were pointed out, accompanied by the triumphant declaration, 'No more Ali Baba!' The famous story of the 40 thieves from *A Thousand and One Nights* was still relevant and being passed down through oral tradition to village children in rural Egypt.

After observing the disturbing effect of the bicycle disaster, our own family's stresses were reprioritised and shrank back down to the smaller categories they deserved. No mere thief could wreck divine faithfulness; it was another intervention of God's presence in the details of life, which could be celebrated.

Burning bush

The sun peered through the smog today.
It lit a tree
aflame.
A burning bush it was to
me.
I AM spoke my
name.

Burning

20

The Middle Eastern carpenter

Our Cairo church fundraising auction for the needy had just proved a major success. This annual money-making dinner also jumpstarted the appearance of our *Spirit of Giving Catalogue*. Many people living in Egypt welcome such a tangible link to help them relieve the suffering they see all around them. When the Christmas season rolls round and you are faced with giving your child's school teacher another apple-themed gift, you can instead fund a 'summer camp for a needy child' in their honour, and know that a little person who would never otherwise see the beach will be ensured a lifelong memory of waves, sand and friendship. What about your father, who has every gadget under the sun? Does he really want another Egyptian souvenir or would he rather receive the gift of having provided 'a year's education for a deaf child' here in Egypt? The list goes on, from paying for help for refugees to increasing a family's livelihood by caring for their donkeys.

Facilitating such projects was a valuable endeavour, unless no donations appeared. Our collection tactic for the first few years was to recruit volunteers for four-hour shifts, sitting at outdoor collection points where people were shopping in the holiday bazaars. Because no snow blows through Egypt we are not equipped with cold climate apparel. After sitting outside here in December, though, even the best dressed of volunteers would be shivering and shaking. No matter how many cups of hot chocolate I consumed, by the end of my shift I would find myself wishing the charity catalogue had never existed. Then, feeling hugely guilty for entertaining such thoughts, I'd try to resort my feelings, eventually deciding that the catalogue wasn't the issue: it was the need for the catalogue, the problem of poverty in the world in general. Meanwhile, the casualty list of volunteer drop-outs grew longer and longer each season, until finally we saw reason and decided that collecting donations in 'lock boxes' was the answer. After all, if the local travel agency here could do it successfully, why couldn't the church?

Security was our primary concern, so plans were drawn up to ensure suitable boxes. Gift cards and catalogues would be placed on narrow shelves attached to the sides of each box. Wood stain of an aesthetically pleasing tone would grace the face of collection and attract concerned contributors to the cause.

Respectful of the fact that we would be working with a Middle Eastern carpenter, a strong male representative of the church—my husband—was recruited to commission the task. As time went on and weeks of delays swept by, however, we began to wonder what had swallowed the tools and time of our skilled employee. Paul-Gordon made multiple diplomatic visits to his shop, employing gentle persuasion techniques, until the final deadline loomed near. The new catalogues had just arrived from the printer so the collecting of contributions could begin; the day of reckoning had arrived.

On the very day of the 'reckoning', I received a phone call from Paul-Gordon. It was almost noon, he had visited the carpenter again, and guess what? The lock boxes were not finished. I was walking home from the corner market at the time and found him standing outside our apartment building, bewildered in the face of yet another crisis. This happened to be the first day of a lecture visit we had organised with a well-known American author, Anne Lamott, and he was due to take her to the first speaking venue. Their meetings that day were all in the congested downtown zone of Cairo where parking options were a dream of the past; a taxi driver was mandatory. On most occasions we simply hailed random taxis—but then we had to risk sitting on age-old seats with only 'natural' air conditioning available. Our usual trusted driver had appeared in good spirits but, when asked if the air conditioner was working, he'd said vaguely that it was now winter. Even if it had been less than 80 degrees Fahrenheit, there would still be traffic exhaust to contend with, and we had to be able to close the windows without suffocating.

I arrived upon the scene of stressful deliberation at just the right moment. I offered to part with our own car for the day and the driver readily agreed. The only major driving I had planned was the trip to the carpenter's shop. How hard could it be to hail one taxi and pick up two charity lock boxes?

As the wooden products were now promised by 4pm, I decided to show cultural grace and appear at 4.30. I was happy to find that my taxi hailing produced a non-smoking driver with airflow controls, as well as unstuck windows that rolled up and down perfectly. It was a beautiful afternoon and I loved the part of town where the carpenter worked. My favourite trees in the world grew next door to his workshop—two banana trees. When I was a young child in Africa, a long line of banana trees surrounded our garden, and the sight of one still invokes happy memories. I emerged from my taxi, asked the driver to wait for me, and found the hardworking carpenter just attaching the doors to our boxes. I smiled and gestured and he laughed in welcome.

'*Malesh* (no problem), Madame Paul,' he beamed. 'Almost finished. Good boxes, yes?'

'Yes, very nice boxes,' I replied.

'Please sit down and wait,' his apprentice offered thoughtfully.

'Thank you so much, but I need to pick up my children. What time should I come back?' I queried, glancing down at my watch.

'One hour maximum. *Malesh*,' he replied.

'Are you sure?' I asked sceptically.

'For sure, Madame,' he smiled jovially. His apprentice nodded in agreement but I silently decided to return no less than two hours later. As I was leaving, I looked next door to soak in the comforting sight of my banana trees. Oddly, there was a crew of people surrounding them, in the midst of a lively discussion. A glimpse of an axe and two hoes confirmed my worst fears. There was nothing wrong with my dusty green trees but I could not prevent their demise. Maybe they were blocking the pavement for passers-by, or there were plans to build on the site. I grieved the needless destruction and headed home in a state of mild gloom.

Two hours later, I reappeared at the carpenter's in another taxi. Refusing to glance at the now barren tree lot, I entered the workshop and found the carpenter grinning and sanding away cheerfully at the boxes as if clocks never existed. Unwisely, I had not anticipated such a possibility, although my husband had warned me. I could think of a different Middle Eastern carpenter—from 2000 years ago—who would certainly have finished this commission on time! Indignantly I wondered what my next approach should be. If I seemed mildly dis- pleased, would he work any faster? Perhaps rage would pick up the pace? Firm grace was what I settled for first. That, and I engaged his apprentice as a witness to the most recently promised completion time.

'Fifteen minutes maximum, Madame,' was the reply. 'Please, sit down, really no problem.'

Did he say 15 minutes to finish the sanding, the staining and the drying process? From what I could see, that would be pushing things, slightly. Watches were synchronised and I promised to return. In one hour I'd be back—maybe two would be safer. My taxi driver ferried me home.

Another two hours later, I appeared at the carpenter's. I had hitched a ride with an older cab driver, who looked like my grandfather but with brown eyes. I felt surprisingly calm upon arrival, and found the carpenter grinning and now staining away cheerfully, as if clocks never existed... He welcomed me warmly, so I asked my driver to wait and graciously took a seat. I was not going to leave the shop without my charity lock boxes in hand.

Finally, the carpenter was at work on the last box. He rubbed and rubbed and rubbed that last box with great precision and pride. He rubbed and smiled and rubbed and hummed. Now I guessed he was testing my patience, to see yet another foreigner break. I leaned back into his hand-crafted chair, determined to relax for the ride. I reckoned that two hours earlier, his '15-minute' promise had probably lost its way among coffee cups and *shee-shaas* (water pipes) and the pure pleasure of celebrating life. As conversation went on, he told me how much he appreciated my husband's kind spirit. A good man—*habibi*, he called him—a compliment reserved for true friends.

I waved to my grandpa driver, who was happy to see time ticking by without effort; I had promised a good wage for his services. By the end of the hour, both boxes were shining and I felt a huge sense of satisfaction. I held success in my hands. The hard-earned accomplishment was a work of art— beautiful, if sticky.

Closer inspection showed minor mistakes, but who couldn't be flexible over those? The carpenter did a final perusal while I pulled a large bag from my purse. Quickly I realised that more dignity was at stake, as the packing job belonged to the apprentice. He refuted my idea to use the plastic as a seat protector; I had forgotten to account for sudden stops and big bumps, he explained. After several false packing starts, all was finally settled. My husband would come to pay later.

I thanked the carpenter for his work and tried to explain the charitable purpose of these boxes. The proud artisan smiled in approval and sent me on my way. The apprentice carefully put the boxes in the taxi and I climbed in next to them for the return journey home. As the car began to pull away, the carpenter came over to add a final contribution.

'May God's peace bless your family, Madame.'

'And yours as well,' I called in return.

A bountiful blessing of grace had been given, the generous gift of a Middle Eastern carpenter.

The gift of grace

If faith is to transform
within,
why do you judge the
outer?
Is the gift of grace
only to save,
or could it guide our lives?

Not a material object

Women are not material objects;
none of your people are.

Do you think our God in heaven
made some superior to others?

We are all children of Abraham,
though centuries have changed.

Our Designer, Creator of the universe—
his children remain the same.

- 21 -

Waste management
redeemers

When I was watering my plants at sunrise one morning, I noticed that the day's air was not just thick, foggy smog soup but smelled of roasted rubbish as well. Yikes! I would not be getting a glimpse of my favourite view—the pyramids across the River Nile—during my drive downtown. Good to note that ahead of time: it's always helpful to premeditate plans in the face of looming triggers of negativity.

Bravely I set off and, as I drove along, flashing billboard signs in my mind invited me to attend the now in-session Complaint Convention. 'No way; don't go there.' I felt instant relief to hear wise counsel coming from within. Every single time I'd been wooed into such a session, I'd found myself exhausted and miserable by the end.

Glancing around as I navigated traffic, I noticed the street cleaners faithfully managing litter and grime with their home-made palm bristle brooms. I blasted past in my air-conditioned protective bubble and a wave of compassion swept over me. Thank goodness I'd turned down the Complaint Convention today. My agenda list vanished completely. How could I ever touch the life of a street sweeper in Cairo? As a woman here, the link was impossible. It was not even appropriate for me to greet them with a smile when I walked past them in the street—though I did anyway. Would I smile at the police on every street corner? No way. They make weird animal-like noises at me, and who wants trouble with the law? But the rubbish collectors and street cleaners were a different story. Our spirits had an understanding.

Back in my car after an uneventful morning, I raced to get home. Several blocks from my destination, a traffic jam suddenly snarled. The man in front of me had jumped out of his car and was screaming wildly at a rubbish truck next to him. Of course, after some years on the job I can now distinguish between playful Middle Eastern drama and human meanness. This was pure meanness. The bewildered driver of the truck craned his neck out of the window. His arm stuck out, too, bearing a makeshift plaster cast. It looked painfully inadequate to correct any possible sort of trauma. There would be chronic pain, for sure. His colleague came round the side of the truck to see what had gone wrong. By now the shouting man's ugly persona had reared its head and its whole body too. He was whipping the other with very harsh words, yelling, gesturing, shaming him—and shaming his Creator in the process. I'd never seen such a docile, broken face, as the rubbish collector apologised. Apparently an empty Coke can had spilled over and hit the man's valuable car. Wow! Could life come to this?

By now, a pack of wedged cars behind me were honking incessantly. I wanted to dash out and hug the dear pummelled man. I also wanted to strangle the one who was violently disgracing humanity. I wonder what he would have done to me if I'd pointed out that his actions were 'forbidden' in Islam? My Arabic failed me just in time as he raced off into the gloom. I waved a thank you to the rubbish truck as it politely let me pass.

Somewhat frazzled and confused, I pulled up in front of my apartment building. I searched in vain for our *boabs* to help unload some heavy items from my car. As I started to carry in my bags, the street sweeper assigned to our neighbourhood came over. He apprehensively gestured his willingness to help me. I knew my *boabs* would veto such a suggestion—too many 'classes' below me, they'd infer. But, since they were nowhere in sight, I eagerly accepted his offer.

The sweeper carefully carried my valuables as far as the building's lift. I tipped him a small thank you gift and he beamed with delight. I'm not sure which we were celebrating—another meal he could provide for his family or the smashing of barriers and greeting of spirits.

Later that day, when I was preparing a church school lesson, I found myself alive in a story of Jesus and all the barriers he had broken. Through the lens of this Middle Eastern culture, his life was radical, multiplied a thousand times. When he told his listeners to invite the poor, the crippled, the lame and the blind to a banquet (Luke 14:12–14), he was describing something impossible. Anyone who was able to throw a party would never consider such a guest list, and the ones who might have these people as their friends could never afford such a luxury. But, he says, although such guests cannot 'repay' you, 'you will be blessed'. He knew from experience. I know why he chose the company he did. It wasn't because of divine requirements or pity; it was because his spirit soared in their presence. He had looked into their eyes, and what he saw there was not waste or a lesser human being. He saw his Father's handprint and loving design.

Just when I thought

Just when I thought the
world had turned hostile,
you
redeemed
the day.

Journal revisited

I am sitting alone in the dining room of our Cairo apartment with the luxury of almost an hour of 'quiet'. I hear a car alarm going off outside, and a train, holding down its horn, has just blown by my front balcony, but my Celtic CD is playing courageously, drowning out the exterior world. The sun is shining this morning. We were even treated briefly to the hint of a baby blue sky and some powdery clouds, after I had endured a night of coughing smoky air, despite the best efforts of my air purifier. The annual Egyptian experience of burning fields following the harvest season is underway.

From where I am sitting, all I can see out of the window is haze, yet I can still see impressions through it. Across the railroad tracks I can glimpse a dust-covered building facing me, and outside there is a mustard yellow bush just in bloom—a striking colour contrast to the surrounding scene. It's another burning bush to me. I sense God's presence and provision of daily bread. Happy sparrows and a pair of laughing doves feed on the seed in my flower boxes. There is our exotic pigeon, Farruk. His feathered feet set him apart, establishing his imagined dominance over the less Pharonic-looking birds. He doesn't fly away when I approach his domain; neither do the doves that we've known since they were hatched. Their mother brought them over to let us celebrate their first winged flight last spring.

Yesterday I came home after taking my children to school,

in a state of major trauma. I had stopped briefly at a little grocer's to buy fruit. As I was leaving, I saw the common sight of a female street dog, but this one was different: her underbelly swollen from nursing, and her leg severely broken. She was limping and dragging it, no doubt having just avoided a fatal car accident. I burst into tears. There wasn't a thing I could do about it, absolutely nothing. In the States I could have rescued her without the likelihood of encountering rabies. In the past, I've paid security guards generously to take in dying kittens, but everyone around here fears dogs. The suffering of animals disturbs me greatly—as, of course, does the human suffering. I struggle with layer upon layer of suffering, with having to digest it helplessly.

Some lessons don't end until you learn from them—really learn, meaning to embrace, embody and accept with gratitude whatever it is that has been grating against your very being. How many times do I have to have my eyes and heart prised open to the reality that I'm still wallowing at the muddy starting line? What are my choices? I have one, I guess. I must keep moving forward—with more thoughtfulness and experience behind me, I hope, even some proven perseverance thrown in, for what it's worth. I've forgotten yet again to celebrate the beauty of smoggy sunrises and sunsets. And what about the many gifts for the journey, not least breath, life, health, family and fellow pilgrims?

Today I think again about how I have been given the generous gift of life in Cairo. Strong, warm arms are handing it to me and I hold my hands open to receive. I let it sit there, not sure what's next. I don't want to unwrap it, right here. I wonder what is inside, though. Maybe it's something just to help me rest, now, in the present moment. Will the Gift-Giver stay with me? Yes—but I don't like this place. Can't I go somewhere else to enjoy the gift? I know the answer already: it will be useless elsewhere. This is a gift for the here and now. It is a gift my Creator noticed I needed. He knows I didn't choose this place. It chose me; he chose me. I was put here and I have to trust him. Will this gift help with that? Yes—but I'm too tired even to pick it up. Can he hold it for me? Yes.

I feel so down and discouraged. Circumstances beyond my control have cut a piece of joy from my soul. What can I do while I'm waiting for time and God's embrace to redeem me?

Today is the day. Now is the moment. The dance of life selects its own lines and rhythms. Join in. The river is flowing: stand by and watch it float away, or step in and start swimming.

Hug back. Be thankful. Focus on God's goodness. Fixate on faithfulness. Let go, listen, love. Maybe even decide to celebrate, throw a party—and invite your heart.

Suffering

I embrace the suffering today has given.
Etch my soul deeper,
Lord.

Blessings don't just accompany joy, ·
but joy is the partner of mindfulness.
I am minded to live my faith as Jesus modelled,
celebrating God in the present.

Looking through eyes of understanding,
I choose compassion and love.
Layers within begin to peel away, until
my core reflects your image.

Teach me to live life abundantly,
generously, thankfully,
joyfully.

A magic cure

If I was told a magic cure
could keep me from
this hour,
I'd pass it by without a thought.
I need to see your
power.

You have tuned my ears

You have tuned my ears to
music,
focused my eyes on
your art.
I taste, I breathe in,
I embrace
your Spirit.
All I touch reflects
your presence.